Tertullian
To Scapula

Tertullian
To Scapula

Tertullian
To Scapula

© Lighthouse Publishing 2018

Tertullian (155 – 240)

Translated by: Rev. S. Thelwall (1834 – 1922)

Revised by: A.M. Overett, B.A., REL. (b. 1960)

All rights reserved. Without limiting the rights under copyright reserved above, no part of this publication may be reproduced, stored in a retrieval system, or transmitted, in any form or by any means (electronic, mechanical, photocopying, recording or otherwise), without the prior written permission of the copyright owner of this book.

Published by
Lighthouse Christian Publishing
SAN 257-4330
5531 Dufferin Drive
Savage, Minnesota, 55378
United States of America

www.lighthousechristianpublishing.com

Tertullian

Introductory Note.

[a.d. 145–220.] When our Lord repulsed the woman of Canaan (Matt. xv. 22) with apparent harshness, he applied to her people the epithet *dogs*, with which the children of Israel had thought it piety to reproach them. When He accepted her faith and caused it to be recorded for our learning, He did something more: He reversed the curse of the Canaanite and showed that the Church was designed "for all people;" Catholic alike for all time and for all sorts and conditions of men.

Thus the North-African Church was loved before it was born: the Good Shepherd was gently leading those "that were with young." Here was the charter of those Christians to be a Church, who then were Canaanites in the land of their father Ham. It is remarkable indeed that among these pilgrims and strangers to the West the first elements of Latin Christianity come into view. Even at the close of the Second Century the Church in Rome is an inconsiderable, though prominent, member of the great confederation of Christian Churches which has its chief seats in Alexandria and Antioch, and of which the entire Literature is Greek. It is an African presbyter who takes from Latin Christendom the reproach of theological and literary barrenness and begins the great work in which, upon his foundations, Cyprian and Augustine built up, with incomparable genius, that Carthaginian School of Christian thought by which Latin Theology was dominated for centuries. It is important to note (1.) that providentially not one of these illustrious doctors died in Communion with the Roman See, pure though it was and venerable at that time; and (2.) that to the works of Augustine the Reformation in Germany and Continental Europe was largely due; while (3.) the *specialties* of the Anglican Reformation were, in like proportion, due to the writings of Tertullian and Cyprian. The hinges of great and controlling destinies for Western Europe and our own America are to be found in the period we are now approaching.

The merest school-boy knows much of the history of Carthage, and how the North Africans became Roman citizens. How they became Christians is not so clear. A melancholy destiny has enveloped Carthage from the outset, and its glory and greatness as a Christian See were transient indeed. It blazed out all at once in Tertullian, after about a century of missionary labours had been exerted upon its creation: and having given a Minucius Felix, an Arnobius and a Lactantius to adorn the earliest period of Western Ecclesiastical learning, in addition to its nobler luminaries, it rapidly declined. At the beginning of the Third Century, at a council presided over by Agrippinus, Bishop of Carthage, there were present not less than seventy bishops of the Province. A period of cruel persecutions followed, and the African Church received a baptism of blood.

Tertullian was born a heathen, and seems to have been educated at Rome, where he probably practiced as a jurisconsult. We may, perhaps, adopt most of the ideas of Allix, as conjecturally probable, and assign his birth to a.d. 145. He became a Christian about 185, and a presbyter about 190. The period of his strict orthodoxy very nearly expires with the century. He lived to an extreme old age, and some suppose even till a.d. 240. More probably we must adopt the date preferred by recent writers, a.d. 220.

It seems to be the fashion to treat of Tertullian as a Montanist, and only incidentally to celebrate his services to the Catholic Orthodoxy of Western Christendom. Were I his biographer I should reverse this course, as a mere act of justice, to say nothing of gratitude to a man of splendid intellect, to whom the filial spirit of Cyprian accorded the loving tribute of a disciple, and whose genius stamped itself upon the very words of Latin theology, and prepared the language for the labors of a Jerome. In creating the Vulgate, and so lifting the Western Churches into a position of intellectual equality with the East, the latter as well as St. Augustine himself were debtors to Tertullian in a degree not to be estimated by any other than the Providential Mind that inspired his brilliant career as a Christian.

In speaking of Tatian I laid the base for what I wished to say of Tertullian. Let God only be their judge; let us gratefully recognize the debt we owe to them. Let us read them, as we read the works of King Solomon. We must, indeed, approve of the discipline of the Primitive Age, which allowed of no compromises. The Church was struggling for existence, and could not permit any man to become her master. The more brilliant the intellect, the more dangerous to the poor Church were its perversions of her Testimony. Before the heathen tribunals, and in the market-places, it would not answer to let Christianity appear double tongued. The orthodoxy of the Church, not less than her children, was undergoing an ordeal of fire. It seems a miracle that her Testimony preserved its unity, and that heresy was branded as such by the instinct of the Faithful. Poor Tertullian was cut off by his own act. The weeping Church might bewail him as David mourned for Absalom, but like David, she could not give the Ark of God into other hands than those of the loyal and the true. I have set the writings of Tertullian in a natural and logical order, so as to aid the student, and to relieve him from the distractions of such an arrangement as one finds in Oehler's edition. Valuable as it is, the practical use of it is irritating and confusing. The reader of that edition may turn to the slightly differing schemes of Neander and Kaye, for a theoretical order of the works; but here he will find a classification which will aid his inquiries. He will find, first, those works which connect with the Apologists of the former volumes of this series: which illustrate the Church's position toward the outside world, the Jews as well as the Gentiles. Next come those works which contend with internal differences and heresies. And then, those which reflect the morals and manners of Christians. These are classed with some reference to their degrees of freedom from the Montanistic taint, and are followed, last of all, by the few tracts which belong to the melancholy period of his lapse, and are directed against the Church's orthodoxy.

Let it be borne in mind, that if this sad close of Tertullian's career cannot be extenuated, the later history of Latin Christianity forbids us to condemn him, in the tones which proceeded from the Virgin Church with authority, and which the law of her testimony and the instinct of self-preservation forced her to utter. Let us reflect that St. Bernard and after him the Schoolmen, whom we so deservedly honor, separated themselves far more absolutely than ever Tertullian did from the orthodoxy of Primitive Christendom. The schism which withdrew the West from Communion with the original seats of Christendom, and from Nicene Catholicity, was formidable beyond all expression, in comparison with Tertullian's entanglements with a delusion which the See of Rome itself had momentarily patronized. Since the Council of Trent, not a theologian of the Latins has been free from organic heresies, compared with which the fanaticism of our author was a trifling aberration. Since the late Council of the Vatican, essential Montanism has become organized in the Latin Churches: for what are the new revelations and oracles of the pontiff but the *deliria* of another claimant to the voice and inspiration of the Paraclete? Poor Tertullian! The sad influences of his decline and folly have been fatally felt in all the subsequent history of the West, but, surely subscribers to the Modern Creed of the Vatican have reason to "speak gently of *their father's* fall." To Döllinger, with the "Old Catholic" remnant only, is left the right to name the Montanists heretics, or to upbraid Tertullian as a lapser from Catholicity.

From Dr. Holmes, I append the following Introductory Notice:

(I.) Quintus Septimius Florens Tertullianus, as our author is called in the mss. of his works, is thus noticed by Jerome in his *Catalogus Scriptorum Ecclesiasticorum:* "Tertullian, a presbyter, the first Latin writer after Victor and Apollonius, was a native of the province of Africa and city of Carthage, the son of a proconsular centurion: he was a man of a sharp and vehement temper, flourished under Severus and Antoninus Caracalla, and wrote numerous works, which (as they are generally known) I think it unnecessary to particularize. I saw at Concordia, in Italy, an old man named Paulus. He said that when young he had met at Rome with an aged amanuensis of the blessed Cyprian, who told him that Cyprian never passed a day without reading some portion of Tertullian's works, and used frequently to say, *Give me my master*, meaning Tertullian. After remaining a presbyter of the church until he had attained the middle age of life, Tertullian was, by the envy and contumelious treatment of the Roman clergy, driven to embrace the opinions of Montanus, which he has mentioned in several of his works under the title of the New Prophecy....He is reported to have lived to a very advanced age, and to have composed many other works which are not extant." We add Bishop Kaye's notes on this extract, in an abridged shape: "The correctness of some parts of this account has been questioned. Doubts have been entertained whether Tertullian was a presbyter, although these have solely arisen from Roman Catholic objections to a married priesthood; for it is certain that he was married, there being among his works two treatises addressed to his wife....Another question has been raised respecting the place where Tertullian officiated as a presbyter—whether at Carthage or at Rome. That he at one time resided at Carthage may be inferred from Jerome's statement, and is rendered certain by several passages of his own writings. Allix supposes that the notion of his having been a presbyter of the Roman Church owed its rise to what Jerome said of the envy and abuse of the Roman clergy impelling him to espouse the party of Montanus. Optatus, and the author of the work *de Hæresibus*, which Sirmond edited under the title of Prædestinatus, expressly call him a Carthaginian presbyter. Semler, however, in a dissertation inserted in his edition of Tertullian's works, contends that he was a presbyter of the Roman Church. Eusebius tells us that he was accurately acquainted with the Roman laws, and on other accounts a distinguished person at Rome. Tertullian displays, moreover, a knowledge of the proceedings of the Roman Church with respect to Marcion and Valentinus, who were once members of it, which could scarcely have been obtained by one who had not himself been numbered amongst its presbyters Semler admits that, after Tertullian seceded from the church, he left and returned to Carthage. Jerome does not inform us whether Tertullian was born of Christian parents, or was converted to Christianity. There are passages in his writings which seem to imply that he had been a Gentile; yet he may perhaps mean to describe, not his own condition, but that of Gentiles in general, before their conversion. Allix and the majority of commentators understand them literally, as well as some other passages in which he speaks of his own infirmities and sinfulness. His writings show that he flourished at the period specified by Jerome—that is, during the reigns of Severus and Antoninus Caracalla, or between the years a.d. 193 and 216; but they supply no precise information respecting the date of his birth, or any of the principal occurrences of his life. Allix places his birth about 145 or 150; his conversion to Christianity about a.d. 185; his marriage about 186; his admission to the priesthood about 192; his adoption of the opinions of Montanus about 199; and his death about a.d. 220.

But these dates, it must be understood, rest entirely on conjecture."

(II.) Tertullian's work against Marcion, as it happens, is, *as to its date*, the best authenticated—perhaps the only well authenticated—particular connected with the author's life.

He himself mentions the fifteenth year of the reign of Severus as the time when he was writing the work: "Ad xv. jam Severi imperatoris." This agrees with Jerome's Chronicle, where occurs this note: "Anno 2223 Severi xv° Tertullianus...celebratur." This year is assigned to the year of our Lord 207; but notwithstanding the certainty of this date, it is far from clear that it describes more than the time of the publication of *the first book*. On the contrary, it is nearly certain that the other books, although connected manifestly enough in the author's argument and purpose (compare the initial and the final chapters of the several books), were yet issued at separate times. Noesselt shows that between the Book i. and Books ii.–iv. Tertullian issued his *De Præscript. Hæret.*, and previous to Book v. he published his tracts, *De Carne Christi* and *De Resurrectione Carnis*. After giving the incontestable date of the xv. of Severus for the first book, he says it is a mistake to suppose that the other books were published with it. He adds: "Although we cannot undertake to determine whether Tertullian issued his Books ii., iii., iv., against Marcion, together or separately, or in what year, we yet venture to affirm that Book v. appeared apart from the rest. For the tract *De Resurr. Carnis* appears from its second chapter to have been published after the tract *De Carne Christi*, in which latter work (chap. vii.) he quotes a passage from the fourth book against Marcion. But in his Book v. against Marcion (chap. x.), he refers to his work *De Resurr. Carnis*; which circumstance makes it evident that Tertullian published his Book v. at a different time from his Book iv. In his Book i. he announces his intention (chap. i.) of some time or other completing his tract *De Præscript. Hæret.*, but in his book *De Carne Christi* (chap. ii.), he mentions how he had completed it,—a conclusive proof that his Book i. against Marcion preceded the other books."

(III.) Respecting Marcion himself, the most formidable heretic who had as yet opposed revealed truth, enough will turn up in this treatise, with the notes which we have added in explanation, to satisfy the reader. It will, however, be convenient to give here a few introductory particulars of him. Tertullian mentions Marcion as being, with Valentinus, in communion with the Church at Rome, "under the episcopate of the blessed Eleutherus." He goes on to charge them with "ever-restless curiosity, with which they infected even the brethren;" and informs us that they were more than once put out of communion—"Marcion, indeed, with the 200 sesterces which he brought into the church." He goes on to say, that "being at last condemned to the banishment of a perpetual separation, they sowed abroad the poisons of their doctrines. Afterwards, when Marcion, having professed penitence, agreed to the terms offered to him, that he should receive reconciliation on condition that he brought back to the church the rest also, whom he had trained up for perdition, he was prevented by death." He was a native of Sinope in Pontus, of which city, according to an account preserved by Epiphanius, which, however, is somewhat doubtful, his father was bishop, and of high character both for his orthodoxy and exemplary practice. He came to Rome soon after the death of Hyginus, probably about a.d. 141 or 142; and soon after his arrival he adopted the heresy of Cerdon.

(IV.) It is an interesting question as to what edition of the Holy Scriptures Tertullian used in his very copious quotations. It may at once be asserted that he did not cite from the Hebrew, although some writers have claimed for him, among his varied learning, a knowledge of the sacred language. Bp. Kaye observes, page 61, n. 1, that "he sometimes speaks as if he was acquainted with Hebrew," and refers to the *Anti-Marcion* iv. 39, the *Adv. Praxeam* v., and the *Adv. Judæos* ix. Be this as it may, it is manifest that Tertullian's Scripture passages never resemble the Hebrew, but in nearly every instance the Septuagint, whenever, as is most frequently the case, that version differs from the original. In the New Testament there is, as might be expected, a tolerably close conformity to the Greek. There is, however, it must be allowed, a sufficiently frequent variation from the letter of both the Greek Testaments to justify Semler's suspicion that Tertullian always quoted from the old Latin version, whatever that might have been, which was current in the African church in the second and third centuries. The most valuable part of Semler's *Dissertatio de varia et incerta indole Librorum Q. S. F. Tertulliani* is his investigation of this very point. In section iv. he endeavors to prove this proposition: "Hic scriptor non in manibus habuit Græcos libros sacros;" and he states his conclusion thus: "Certissimum est nec Tertullianum nec Cyprianum nec ullum scriptorem e Latinis illis ecclesiasticis provocare unquam ad Græcorum librorum auctoritatem si vel maxime obscura aut contraria lectio occurreret;" and again: "Ex his satis certum est, Latinos satis diu secutos fuisse auctoritatem suorum librorum adversus Græcos, nec concessisse nisi serius, cum Augustini et Hieronymi nova auctoritas juvare videretur." It is not ignorance of Greek which is imputed to Tertullian, for he is said to have well understood that language, and even to have composed in it. He probably followed the Latin, as writers now usually quote the authorized English, as being current and best known among their readers. Independent feeling, also, would have weight with such a temper as Tertullian's, to say nothing of the suspicion which largely prevailed in the African branch of the Latin church, that the Greek copies of the Scriptures were much corrupted by the heretics, who were chiefly, if not wholly, Greeks or Greek-speaking persons.

(V.) Whatever perverting effect Tertullian's secession to the sect of Montanus may have had on his judgment in his latest writings, it did not vitiate the work against Marcion. With a few trivial exceptions, this treatise may be read by the strictest Catholic without any feeling of annoyance. His lapse to Montanism is set down conjecturally as having taken place a.d. 199. Jerome, we have seen, attributed the event to his quarrel with the Roman clergy, but this is at least doubtful; nor must it be forgotten that Tertullian's mind seems to have been peculiarly suited by nature to adopt the mystical notions and ascetic principles of Montanus. It is satisfactory to find that, on the whole, "the authority of Tertullian," as the learned Dr. Burton says, "upon great points of doctrine is considered to be little, if at all, affected by his becoming a Montanist." (*Lectures on Eccl. Hist.* vol. ii. p. 234.) Besides the different works which are expressly mentioned in the notes of this volume, recourse has been had by the translator to Dupin's *Hist. Eccl. Writers* (trans.), vol. i. pp. 69–86; Tillemont's *Mèmoires Hist. Eccl.* iii. 85–103; Dr. Smith's *Greek and Roman Biography*, articles "Marcion" and "Tertullian;" Schaff's article, in Herzog's *Cyclopædia*, on "Tertullian;" Munter's *Primordia Eccl. Africanæ*, pp. 118–150; Robertson's *Church Hist.* vol. i. pp. 70–77; Dr. P. Schaff's *Hist. of Christian Church* (New York, 1859, pp. 511–519), and Archdeacon Evans' *Biography of the Early Church*, vol. i. (Lives of "Marcion," pp. 93–122, and "Tertullian," pp. 325–363). This last work, though of a popular cast, shows a good deal of research and learning, expressed in the pleasant style of the once popular author of *The Rectory of Vale Head*. The translator has mentioned these works, because they are all quite accessible to the general reader, and will give him adequate information concerning the subject treated in the present volume.

To this introduction of Dr. Holmes must be added that of Mr. Thelwall, the translator of the Third volume in the Edinburgh Series, as follows:

To arrange chronologically the works (especially if numerous) of an author whose own date is known with tolerable precision, is not always or necessarily easy: witness the controversies as to the succession of St. Paul's epistles. To do this in the case of an author whose own date is itself a matter of controversy may therefore be reasonably expected to be still less so; and such is the predicament of him who attempts to perform this task for Tertullian. I propose to give a specimen or two of the difficulties with which the task is beset; and then to lay before the reader briefly a summary of the results at which eminent scholars, who have devoted much time and thought to the subject, have arrived. Such a course, I think, will at once afford him means of judging of the absolute impossibility of arriving at definite certainty in the matter; and induce him to excuse me if I prefer furnishing him with materials from which to deduce his own conclusions, rather than venturing on an *ex cathedra* decision on so doubtful a subject.

I. The book, as Dr. Holmes has reminded us, of the date of which we seem to have the surest evidence, is *Adv. Marc.* i. This book was in course of writing, as its author himself (c. 15) tells us, "in the fifteenth year of the empire of Severus." Now this date would be clear if there were no doubt as to which year of our era corresponds to Tertullian's fifteenth of Severus. Pamelius, however, says Dr. Holmes, makes it a.d. 208; Clinton, (whose authority is more recent and better,) 207.

2. Another book which promises to give some clue to its date is the *de Pallio*. The writer uses these phrases: "præsentis imperii *triplex virtus*;" "Deo *tot Augustis in unum* favente;" which show that there were at the time three persons unitedly bearing the title *Augusti*—not *Cæsares* only, but the still higher *Augusti*;—while the remainder of that context, as well as the opening of c. 1, indicates a time of peace of some considerable duration; a time of plenty; and a time during and previous to which great changes had taken place in the general aspect of the Roman Empire, and some particular traitor had been discovered and frustrated. Such a combination of circumstances might seem to fix the date with some degree of assurance. But unhappily, as Kaye reminds us, commentators cannot agree as to who the three Augusti are. Some say

Severus, Caracalla, and *Albinus*; some say Severus, Caracalla, and *Geta*. Hence we have a difference of some twelve years or thereabouts in the computations. For Albinus was defeated by Severus in person, and fell by his own hand, in a.d. 197; and Geta, Severus' second son, brother of Caracalla, was not associated by his father with himself and his other son as *Augustus* until a.d. 208, though he had received the title of *Cæsar* ten years before, in the same year in which *Caracalla* had received that of Augustus. For my own part, I may perhaps be allowed to say that I should incline to agree, like Salmasius, with those who assign the later date. The limits of the present Introduction forbid my entering at large into my reasons for so doing. I am, however, supported in it by the authority of Neander. In one point, though, I should hesitate to agree with Oehler, who appears to follow Salmasius and others herein,— namely, in understanding the expression "et cacto et rubo subdolæ familiaritatis convulso" of *Albinus*. It seems to me the words might with more propriety be applied to *Plautianus*; and that in the word "familiaritatis" we may see (after Tertullian's fashion) a play upon the meaning, with a reference not only to the long-standing but mischievous *intimacy* which existed between Severus and his countryman (perhaps fellow-townsman) Plautianus, who for his harshness and cruelty is fitly compared to the prickly *cactus*. He alludes likewise to the alliance which this ambitious prætorian præfect had contrived to contract with the *family* of the emperor, by the marriage of his daughter Plautilla to Caracalla,—an event which, as it turned out, led to his own death. Thus in the *"rubo"* there may be a reference to the ambitious and conceited "bramble" of Jotham's parable, and perhaps, too, to the "thistle" of Jehoash's. If this be so, the date would be at least approximately fixed, as Plautianus did not marry his daughter to Caracalla till a.d. 203, and was himself put to death in the following year, 204, while Geta, as we have seen, was made Augustus in 208.

3. The date of the *Apology*, however, is perhaps at once the most contested, and the most strikingly illustrative of the difficulties to which allusion has been made. It is not surprising that its date *should* have been more disputed than that of other pieces, inasmuch as it is the best known, and (for some reasons) the most interesting and famous, of all our author's productions. In fact, the dates assigned to it by different authorities vary from Mosheim's 198 to that suggested by the very learned Allix, who assigns it to 217.

4. Once more. In the tract *de Monogamia* (c. 3) the author says that since the date of St. Paul's first Epistle to the Corinthians "about 160 years had elapsed." Here, again, did we only know with certainty the precise date of that epistle, we could ascertain "about" the date of the tract. But (a) the date of the epistle is itself variously given, Burton giving it as early as a.d. 52, Michaelis and Mill as late as 57; and (b) Tertullian only says, "Armis *circiter* clx. exinde productis;" while the way in which, in the *ad Natt.*, within the short space of three chapters, he states first that 250, and then (in c. 9) that 300, years had not elapsed since the rise of the Christian name, leads us to think that here again he only desires to speak in round numbers, meaning perhaps *more* than 150, but *less* than 170.

These specimens must suffice, though it might be easy to add to them. There is, however, another classification of our author's writings which has been attempted. Finding the haplessness of strict chronological accuracy, commentators have seized on the idea that peradventure there might be found at all events some internal marks by which to determine which of them were written before, which after, the writer's secession to Montanism. It may be confessed that this attempt has been somewhat more successful than the other. Yet even here there are two formidable obstacles standing in our way. The first and greatest is, that the natural temper of Tertullian was from the first so akin to the spirit of Montanism, that, unless there occur distinct allusions to the "New Prophecy," or expressions specially connected with Montanistic phraseology, the *general tone* of any treatise is not a very safe guide. The second is, that the subject-matter of some of the treatises is not such as to afford much scope for the introduction of the peculiarities of a sect which professed to differ in discipline only, not doctrine, from the church at large.

Still the result of this classification seems to show one important feature of agreement between commentators, however they may differ upon details; and that is, that considerably the larger part of our author's rather voluminous productions must have been subsequent to his lamented secession. I think the best way to give the reader means for forming his own judgment will be, as I have said, to lay before him in parallel columns a tabular view of the disposition of the books by Dr. Neander and Bishop Kaye. These two modern writers, having given particular care to the subject, bringing to bear upon it all the advantages derived from wide reading, eminent abilities, and a diligent study of the works of preceding writers on the same questions, have a special right to be heard upon the matter in hand; and I think, if I may be allowed to say so, that, for calm judgment, and minute acquaintance with his author, I shall not be accused of undue partiality if I express my opinion that, as far as my own observation goes, the palm must be awarded to the Bishop. In this view I am supported by the fact that the accomplished Professor Ramsay, follows Dr. Kaye's arrangement. I premise that Dr. Neander adopts a threefold division, into:

1. Writings which were occasioned by the relation of the Christians to the heathen, and refer to their vindication of Christianity against the heathen; attacks on heathenism; the sufferings and conduct of Christians under persecution; and the intercourse of Christians with heathens:
2. Writings which relate to Christian and church life, and to ecclesiastical discipline:
3. The dogmatic and dogmatico-controversial treatises.
And under each head he subdivides into:

a. Pre-Montanist writings; b. Post-Montanist writings: thus leaving no room for what Kaye calls "works respecting which nothing certain can be pronounced." For the sake of clearness, this order has not been followed in the table. On the other side, it will be seen that Dr. Kaye, while not assuming to speak with more than a reasonable probability, is careful so to arrange the treatises under each head as to show the order, so far as it is discoverable, in which the books under that head were published; i.e., if one book is quoted in another book, the book so quoted, if distinctly referred to as already before the world, is plainly anterior to that in which it is quoted. Thus, then, have:

Neander.
I. *Pre-Montanist.*
1. De Poenitentia.
2. De Oratione.
3. De Baptismo.
4. Ad Uxorem i.
5. Ad Uxorem ii.
6. Ad Martyres.
7. De Patientia.
8. De Spectaculis.
9. De Idololatria.
10. 11. Ad Nationes i. ii.
12. Apologeticus.
13. De Testimonio Animæ.
14. De Præscr. Hæreticorum.
15. De Cult. Fem. i.
16. De Cult. Fem. ii.
II. *Montanist.*
17–21. Adv. Marc. i. ii. iii. iv. v.
22. De Anima.
23. De Carne Christi.
24. De Res. Carn.
25. De Cor. Mil.

26. De Virg. Vel.
27. De Ex. Cast.
28. De Monog.
29. De Jejuniis.
30. De Pudicitia.
31. De Pallio.
32. Scorpiace.
33. Ad Scapulam.
34. Adv. Valentinianos.
35. Adv. Hermogenem.
36. Adv. Praxeam.
37. Adv. Judæos.
38. De Fuga in Persecutione.
Kaye.
I. *Pre-Montanist* (probably).
1. De Poenitentia.
2. De Oratione.
3. De Baptismo.
4. Ad Uxorem i.
5. Ad Uxorem ii.
6. Ad Martyres.
7. De Patientia.
8. Adv. Judæos.
9. De Præscr. Hæreticorum.
II. *Montanist* (certainly).
10. Adv. Marc. i.
11. Adv. Marc. ii.
12. De Anima.
13. Adv. Marc. iii.
14. Adv. Marc. iv.
15. De Carne Christi.
16. De Resurrectione Carnis.
17. Adv. Marc. v.
18. Adv. Praxeam.
19. Scorpiace.
20. De Corona Militis.

21. De Virginibus Velandis.
22. De Exhortatione Castitatis.
23. De Fuga in Persecutione.
24. De Monogamia.
25. De Jejuniis.
26. De Pudicitia.
III. *Montanist* (probably).
27. Adv. Valentinianos.
28. Ad Scapulam.
29. De Spectaculis.
30. De Idololatria.
31. De Cultu Feminarum i.
32. De Cultu Feminarum ii.
IV. *Works respecting which nothing certain can be pronounced.*
33. The Apology.
34. Ad Nationes i.
35. Ad Nationes ii.
36. De Testimonio Animæ.
37. De Pallio.
38. Adv. Hermogenem.

A comparison of these two lists will show that the difference between the two great authorities is, as Kaye remarks, "not great; and with respect to some of the tracts on which we differ, the learned author expresses himself with great diffidence." The main difference, in fact, is that which affects two tracts upon kindred subjects, the *de Spectaculis*, and *Idololatria*, the *de Cultu Feminarum* (a subject akin to the other two), and the *adv. Judæos*. With reference to all these, except the last, to which I believe the Archdeacon does not once refer, the Bishop's opinion appears to have the support of Archdeacon Evans, whose learned and interesting essay, referred to in the note, appears in a volume published in 1837. Dr. Kaye's Lectures, on which his book is founded, were delivered in 1825. Of the date of his first edition I am not aware. Dr. Neander's *Antignostikus* also first appeared in 1825.

The preface to his second edition bears date July 1, 1849. As to the *adv. Judæos*, I confess I agree with Neander in thinking that, at all events from the beginning of c. 9, it is spurious. If it be urged that Jerome expressly quotes it as Tertullian's, I reply, Jerome so quotes it, I believe, when he is expounding *Daniel*. Now all that the *adv. Jud.* has to say about *Daniel* ends with the end of c. 8. It is therefore quite compatible with the fact thus stated to recognize the earlier half of the book as genuine, and to reject the rest, beginning, as it happens, just after the eighth chapter, as spurious. Perhaps Dr. Neander's Jewish birth and training peculiarly fit him to be heard on this question. Nor do I think Professor Ramsay (in the article above alluded to) has quite seen the force of Kaye's own remarks on Neander. What he does say is equally creditable to his candor and his accuracy; namely: "The instances alleged by Dr. Neander, in proof of this position, are undoubtedly very remarkable; but if the concluding chapters of the tract are spurious, no ground seems to be left for asserting that the genuine portion was posterior to the third Book against Marcion,—and none, consequently, for asserting that it was written by a Montanist." With which remark I must draw these observations on the genuine extant works of Tertullian to a close.

The next point to which a brief reference must be made is the *lost works* of Tertullian, lists of these are given both by Oehler and by Kaye, viz.:

1. A Book on Aaron's Robes: mentioned by Jerome, Epist. 128, *ad Fabiolam de Veste Sacerdotali* (tom. ii. p. 586, Opp. ed. Bened.).
2. A Book on the Superstition of the Age.
3. A Book on the Submission of the Soul.
4. A Book on the Flesh and the Soul.

Nos. 2, 3, and 4 are known only by their titles, which are found in the Index to Tertullian's works given in the *Codex Agobardi*; but the tracts themselves are not extant in the ms., which appears to have once contained—

5. A Book on Paradise, named in the Index, and referred to in *de Anima* 55, *adv. Marc.* iii. 12; and

6. A Book on the Hope of the Faithful: also named in the Index, and referred to *adv. Marc.* iii. 24; and by Jerome in his account of Papias, and on Ezek. xxxvi.; and by Gennadius of Marseilles.

7. Six Books on Ecstasy, with a seventh in reply to Apollonius: see Jerome. See, too, J. A. Fabricius on the words of the unknown author whom the Jesuit Sirmond edited under the name *Prædestinatus*; who gathers thence that "Soter, pope of the City, and Apollonius, bishop of the Ephesians, wrote a book against the Montanists; *in reply to whom* Tertullian, a Carthaginian presbyter, wrote." J. Pamelius thinks these seven books were originally published *in Greek*.

8. A Book in reply to the Apellesites (i.e. the followers of Apelles): referred to in *de Carne Christi*, c. 8.

9. A Book on the Origin of the Soul, in reply to Hermogenes: referred to in *de Anima*, cc. 1, 3, 22, 24.

10. A Book on Fate: referred to by Fulgentius Planciades, p. 562, Merc.; also referred to as either written, or intended to be written, by Tertullian himself, *de Anima*, c. 20. Jerome states that there was extant, or had been extant, a book on Fate under the name of Minucius Felix, written indeed by a perspicuous author, but not in the style of Minucius Felix. This, Pamelius judged, should perhaps be rather ascribed to Tertullian.

11. A Book on the Trinity. Jerome says: "Novatian wrote....a large volume on the Trinity, *as if making an epitome of a work of Tertullian's, which most men not knowing regard it as Cyprian's.*" Novatian's book stood in Tertullian's name in the mss. of J. Gangneius, who was the first to edit it; in a Malmesbury ms. which Sig. Gelenius used; and in others.

12. A Book addressed to a Philosophic Friend on the Straits of Matrimony. Both Kaye and Oehler are in doubt whether Jerome's words, by which some have been led to conclude that Tertullian wrote some book or books on this and kindred subjects, really imply as much, or whether they may

not refer merely to those tracts and passages in his extant writings which touch upon such matters. Kaye hesitates to think that the "Book to a Philosophic Friend" is the same as the *de Exhortatione Castitatis,* because Jerome says Tertullian wrote on the subject of celibacy *"in his youth;"* but as Cave takes what Jerome elsewhere says of Tertullian's leaving the Church *"about the middle of his age"* to mean his *spiritual age,* the same sense might attach to his words here too, and thus obviate the Bishop's difficulty.

There are some other works which have been attributed to Tertullian—on Circumcision; on Animals Clean and Unclean; on the truth that God is a Judge—which Oehler likewise rejects, believing that the expressions of Jerome refer only to passages in the *Anti-Marcion* and other extant works. To Novatian Jerome does ascribe a distinct work on Circumcision, and this may (comp. 11, just above) have given rise to the view that Tertullian had written one also.

There were, moreover, three treatises at least written by Tertullian *in Greek.* They are:

1. A Book on Public Shows. See *de Cor.* c. 6.
2. A Book on Baptism. See *de Bapt.* c. 15.
3. A Book on the Veiling of Virgins. See de *V. V.* c. 1.

Oehler adds that J. Pamelius, in his epistle dedicatory to Philip II. of Spain, makes mention of a *Greek copy* of Tertullian in the library of that king. This report, however, since nothing has ever been seen or heard of the said copy from that time, Oehler judges to be erroneous.

It remains briefly to notice the confessedly spurious works which the editions of Tertullian generally have appended to them. With these Kaye does not deal. The fragment, *adv. omnes Hæreses,* Oehler attributes to Victorinus Petavionensis, i.e., Victorinus bishop of Pettaw, on the Drave, in Austrian Styria. It was once thought he ought to be called *Pictaviensis,* i.e. of *Poictiers;* but John Launoy has shown this to be an error. Victorinus is said by Jerome to have "understood Greek better than Latin; hence his works are excellent for the sense, but mean as to the style." Cave believes him to have been a Greek by birth. Cassiodorus states him to have been once a professor of rhetoric. Jerome's statement agrees with the style of the tract in question; and Jerome distinctly says Victorinus did write *adversus omnes Hæreses*. Allix leaves the question of its authorship quite uncertain. If Victorinus be the author, the book falls clearly within the Ante-Nicene period; for Victorinus fell a martyr in the Diocletian persecution, probably about a.d. 303.

The next fragment—"Of the Execrable Gods of the Heathens"—is of quite uncertain authorship. Oehler would attribute it "to some declaimer not quite ignorant of Tertullian's writings," but certainly not to Tertullian himself.

Lastly we come to the metrical fragments. Concerning these, it is perhaps impossible to assign them to their rightful owners. Oehler has not troubled himself much about them; but he seems to regard the *Jonah* as worthy of more regard than the rest, for he seems to have intended giving more labor to its editing at some future time. Whether he has ever done so, or given us his German version of Tertullian's own works, which, "si Deus adjuverit," he distinctly promises in his preface, I do not know. Perhaps the best thing to be done under the circumstances is to give the judgment of the learned Peter Allix. It may be premised that by the celebrated George Fabricius—who published his great work, *Poetarum Veterum Ecclesiasticorum Opera Christiana*, etc., in 1564—the *Five Books in Reply to Marcion*, and the *Judgment of the Lord*, are ascribed to Tertullian, the *Genesis* and *Sodom* to Cyprian.
Pamelius likewise seems to have ascribed the *Five Books*, the *Jonah*, and the *Sodom* to Tertullian; and according to Lardner, Bishop Bull likewise attributed the *Five Books* to him. They have been generally ascribed to the Victorinus above mentioned. Tillemont, among others, thinks they may well enough be his. Rigaltius is content to demonstrate that they are not Tertullian's, but leaves the real authorship without attempting to decide it. Of the others the same eminent critic says, "They seem to have been written at Carthage, at an age

not far removed from Tertullian's." Allix, after observing that Pamelius is inconsistent with himself in attributing the *Genesis* and *Sodom* at one time to Tertullian, at another to
Cyprian, rejects both views equally, and assigns the Genesis with some confidence to Salvian, a presbyter of Marseilles, whose "floruit" Cave gives *cir.* 440, a contemporary of Gennadius, and a copious author. To this it is, Allix thinks, that Gennadius alludes in his *Catalogue of Illustrious Men*, c. 77.

The *Judgment of the Lord* Allix ascribes to one Verecundus, an African bishop, whose date he finds it difficult to decide exactly. He refers to two of the name: one Bishop of Tunis, whom Victor of Tunis in his chronicle mentions as having died in exile at Chalcedon a.d. 552; the other Bishop of Noba, who visited Carthage with many others a.d. 482, at the summons of King Huneric, to answer there for their faith;—and would ascribe the poem to the former, thinking that he finds an allusion to it in the article upon that Verecundus in the *de Viris Illustribus* of Isidore of Seville. Oehler agrees with him. The *Five Books* Allix seems to hint may be attributed to some imitator of the Victorinus of Pettaw named above.

Oehler attributes them rather to one Victorinus, or Victor, of Marseilles, a rhetorician, who died a.d. 450. He appears in G. Fabricius as Claudius Marius Victorinus, writer of a *Commentary on Genesis*, and an epistle *ad Salomonem Abbata*, both in verse, and of some considerable length.

To Scapula.

Chapter I.

We are not in any great perturbation or alarm about the persecutions we suffer from the ignorance of men; for we have attached ourselves to this sect, fully accepting the terms of its covenant, so that, as men whose very lives are not their own, we engage in these conflicts, our desire being to obtain God's promised rewards, and our dread lest the woes with which He threatens an unchristian life should overtake us. Hence we shrink not from the grapple with your utmost rage, coming even forth of our own accord to the contest; and condemnation gives us more pleasure than acquittal. We have sent, therefore, this tract to you in no alarm about ourselves, but in much concern for you and for all our enemies, to say nothing of our friends. For our religion commands us to love even our enemies, and to pray for those who persecute us, aiming at a perfection all its own, and seeking in its disciples something of a higher type than the commonplace goodness of the world. For all love those who love them; it is peculiar to Christians alone to love those that hate them. Therefore mourning over your ignorance, and compassionating human error, and looking on to that future of which every day shows threatening signs, necessity is laid on us to come forth in this way also, that we may set before you the truths you will not listen to openly.

Chapter II.

We are worshippers of one God, of whose existence and character Nature teaches all men; at whose lightnings and thunders you tremble, whose benefits minister to your happiness. You think that others, too, are gods, whom we know to be devils. However, it is a fundamental human right, a

To Scapula

privilege of nature, that every man should worship according to his own convictions: one man's religion neither harms nor helps another man. It is assuredly no part of religion to compel religion—to which free-will and not force should lead us—the sacrificial victims even being required of a willing mind. You will render no real service to your gods by compelling us to sacrifice. For they can have no desire of offerings from the unwilling, unless they are animated by a spirit of contention, which is a thing altogether undivine. Accordingly the true God bestows His blessings alike on wicked men and on His own elect; upon which account He has appointed an eternal judgment, when both thankful and unthankful will have to stand before His bar. Yet you have never detected us—sacrilegious wretches though you reckon us to be—in any theft, far less in any sacrilege. But the robbers of your temples, all of them swear by your gods, and worship them; they are not Christians, and yet it is they who are found guilty of sacrilegious deeds. We have not time to unfold in how many other ways your gods are mocked and despised by their own votaries. So, too, treason is falsely laid to our charge, though no one has ever been able to find followers of Albinus, or Niger, or Cassius, among Christians; while the very men who had sworn by the genii of the emperors, who had offered and vowed sacrifices for their safety, who had often pronounced condemnation on Christ's disciples, are till this day found traitors to the imperial throne. A Christian is enemy to none, least of all to the Emperor of Rome, whom he knows to be appointed by his God, and so cannot but love and honour; and whose well-being moreover, he must needs desire, with that of the empire over which he reigns so long as the world shall stand—for so long as that shall Rome continue. To the emperor, therefore, we render such reverential homage as is lawful for us and good for him; regarding him as the human being next to God who from God has received all his power, and is less than God alone. And this will be according to his own desires. For thus—as less only than the true God—he is greater than all besides. Thus he is greater than the very gods themselves, even they, too, being subject to him. We therefore sacrifice for the emperor's safety, but to our God and his, and after the manner God has enjoined, in simple prayer. For God, Creator of the universe, has no need of odours or of blood. These things are the food of devils. But we not only reject those wicked spirits: we overcome them; we daily hold them up to contempt; we exorcise them from their victims, as multitudes can testify. So all the more we pray for the imperial well-being, as those who seek it at the hands of Him who is able to bestow it. And one would think it must be abundantly clear to you that the religious system under whose rules we act is one inculcating a divine patience; since, though our numbers are so great—constituting all but the majority in every city— we conduct ourselves so quietly and modestly; I might perhaps say, known rather as individuals than as organized communities, and remarkable only for the reformation of our former vices. For far be it from us to take it ill that we have laid on us the very things we wish, or in any way plot the vengeance at our own hands, which we expect to come from God.

Chapter III.

However, as we have already remarked, it cannot but distress us that no state shall bear unpunished the guilt of shedding Christian blood; as you see, indeed, in what took place during the presidency of Hilarian, for when there had been some agitation about places of sepulture for our dead, and the cry arose, "No *areæ*—no burial-grounds for the Christians," it came that their own *areæ*, their threshing-floors, were a-wanting, for they gathered in no harvests. As to the rains of the bygone year, it is abundantly plain of what they were intended to remind men—of the deluge, no doubt, which in ancient times overtook human unbelief and wickedness; and as to the fires which lately hung all night over the walls of

Carthage, they who saw them know what they threatened; and what the preceding thunders pealed, *they* who were hardened by them can tell. All these things are signs of God's impending wrath, which we must needs publish and proclaim in every possible way; and in the meanwhile we must pray it may be only local. Sure are *they* to experience it one day in its universal and final form, who interpret otherwise these samples of it. That sun, too, in the metropolis of Utica, with light all but extinguished, was a portent which could not have occurred from an ordinary eclipse, situated as the lord of day was in his height and house. You have the astrologers, consult them about it. We can point you also to the deaths of some provincial rulers, who in their last hours had painful memories of their sin in persecuting the followers of Christ. Vigellius Saturninus, who first here used the sword against us, lost his eyesight. Claudius Lucius Herminianus in Cappadocia, enraged that his wife had become a Christian, had treated the Christians with great cruelty: well, left alone in his palace, suffering under a contagious malady, he boiled out in living worms, and was heard exclaiming, "Let nobody know of it, lest the Christians rejoice, and Christian wives take encouragement." Afterwards he came to see his error in having tempted so many from their stedfastness by the tortures he inflicted, and died almost a Christian himself. In that doom which overtook Byzantium, Cæcilius Capella could not help crying out, "Christians, rejoice!" Yes, and the persecutors who seem to themselves to have acted with impunity shall not escape the day of judgment. For you we sincerely wish it may prove to have been a warning only, that, immediately after you had condemned Mavilus of Adrumetum to the wild beasts, you were overtaken by those troubles, and that even now for the same reason you are called to a blood-reckoning. But do not forget the future.

Chapter IV.

We who are without fear ourselves are not seeking to frighten you, but we would save all men if possible by warning them not to fight with God. You may perform the duties of your charge, and yet remember the claims of humanity; if on no other ground than that you are liable to punishment yourself, (you ought to do so). For is not your commission simply to condemn those who confess their guilt, and to give over to the torture those who deny? You see, then, how you trespass yourselves against your instructions to wring from the confessing a denial. It is, in fact, an acknowledgment of our innocence that you refuse to condemn us at once when we confess. In doing your utmost to extirpate us, if that is your object, it is innocence you assail. But how many rulers, men more resolute and more cruel than you are, have contrived to get quit of such causes altogether,—as Cincius Severus, who himself suggested the remedy at Thysdris, pointing out how the Christians should answer that they might secure an acquittal; as Vespronius Candidus, who dismissed from his bar a Christian, on the ground that to satisfy his fellow-citizens would break the peace of the community; as Asper, who, in the case of a man who gave up his faith under slight infliction of the torture, did not compel the offering of sacrifice, having owned before, among the advocates and assessors of court, that he was annoyed at having had to meddle with such a case. Pudens, too, at once dismissed a Christian who was brought before him, perceiving from the indictment that it was a case of vexatious accusation; tearing the document in pieces, he refused so much as to hear him without the presence of his accuser, as not being consistent with the imperial commands. All this might be officially brought under your notice, and by the very advocates, who are themselves also under obligations to us, although in court they give their voice as it suits them. The clerk of one of them who was liable to be thrown upon the ground by an evil spirit, was set free from his affliction; as was also the relative

To Scapula

of another, and the little boy of a third. How many men of rank (to say nothing of common people) have been delivered from devils, and healed of diseases! Even Severus himself, the father of Antonine, was graciously mindful of the Christians; for he sought out the Christian Proculus, surnamed Torpacion, the steward of Euhodias, and in gratitude for his having once cured him by anointing, he kept him in his palace till the day of his death. Antonine, too, brought up as he was on Christian milk, was intimately acquainted with this man. Both women and men of highest rank, whom Severus knew well to be Christians, were not merely permitted by him to remain uninjured; but he even bore distinguished testimony in their favour, and gave them publicly back to us from the hands of a raging populace.

Marcus Aurelius also, in his expedition to Germany, by the prayers his Christian soldiers offered to God, got rain in that well-known thirst. When, indeed, have not droughts been put away by our kneelings and our fastings? At times like these, moreover, the people crying to "the God of gods, the alone Omnipotent," under the name of Jupiter, have borne witness to our God. Then we never deny the deposit placed in our hands; we never pollute the marriage bed; we deal faithfully with our wards; we give aid to the needy; we render to none evil for evil. As for those who falsely pretend to belong to us, and whom we, too, repudiate, let them answer for themselves. In a word, who has complaint to make against us on other grounds? To what else does the Christian devote himself, save the affairs of his own community, which during all the long period of its existence no one has ever proved guilty of the incest or the cruelty charged against it? It is for freedom from crime so singular, for a probity so great, for righteousness, for purity, for faithfulness, for truth, for the living God, that we are consigned to the flames; for this is a punishment you are not wont to inflict either on the sacrilegious, or on undoubted public enemies, or on the treason-tainted, of whom you have so many. Nay, even now our people are enduring persecution from the governors of Legio and Mauritania; but it is only with the sword, as from the first it was ordained that we should suffer. But the greater our conflicts, the greater our rewards.

Chapter V.

Your cruelty is our glory. Only see you to it, that in having such things as these to endure, we do not feel ourselves constrained to rush forth to the combat, if only to prove that we have no dread of them, but on the contrary, even invite their infliction. When Arrius Antoninus was driving things hard in Asia, the whole Christians of the province, in one united band, presented themselves before his judgment-seat; on which, ordering a few to be led forth to execution, he said to the rest, "O miserable men, if you wish to die, you have precipices or halters." If we should take it into our heads to do the same thing here, what will you make of so many thousands, of such a multitude of men and women, persons of every sex and every age and every rank, when they present themselves before you? How many fires, how many swords will be required? What will be the anguish of Carthage itself, which you will have to decimate, as each one recognises there his relatives and companions, as he sees there it may be men of your own order, and noble ladies, and all the leading persons of the city, and either kinsmen or friends of those of your own circle? Spare thyself, if not us poor Christians! Spare Carthage, if not thyself! Spare the province, which the indication of your purpose has subjected to the threats and extortions at once of the soldiers and of private enemies. *We* have no master but God. *He is before* you, and cannot be hidden from you, but to Him you can do no injury. But those whom you regard as masters are only men, and one day they themselves must die. Yet still this community will be undying, for be assured that just in the time of its seeming overthrow it is built up into greater power. For all who witness the noble patience of its martyrs, as struck with misgivings, are inflamed with desire to examine into the matter in question; and as soon as they come to know the truth, they straightway enrol themselves its disciples.

Elucidations.

I.

(Scapula, cap. i., p. 105.)

Scapula was Proconsul of Carthage, and though its date is conjectural (a.d. 217), this work gives valuable *indices* of its time and circumstances. It was composed after the death of Severus, to whom there is an allusion in chapter iv., after the destruction of Byzantium (a.d. 196), to which there is a reference in chapter iii.; and Dr. Allix suggests, after the dark day of Utica (a.d. 210) which he supposes to be referred to in the same chapter. Cincius Severus, who is mentioned in chapter iv., was put to death by Severus, a.d. 198.

II.

(Caractacus, cap. ii., note 2, p. 105.)

Mr. Lewin (*St. Paul*, ii. 397), building on the fascinating theory of Archdeacon Williams, thinks St. Paul's Claudia (*Qu. Gladys?*) may very well have been the daughter of Caradoc, with whose noble character we are made acquainted by Tacitus. (Annals xii. 36.) And Archdeacon Williams gives us very strong reason to believe he was a Christian. He may very well have lived to behold the Coliseum completed. What more natural then, in view of the cruelty against Christians there exercised, for the expressions with which he is credited? In this case his words contain an eloquent ambiguity, which Christians would appreciate, and which may have been in our author's mind when he says—"quousque sæculum stabit." To those who looked for the Second Advent, daily, this did not mean what the heathen might suppose.

Bede's version of the speech (See Du Cange, II., 407.,) is this: "Quandiu stabit Colyseus—stabit et Roma: Quando cadet Colysevs—cadet et Roma: Quando cadet Roma—cadet et mundus."